A growing list of your author's books
are attached in the back of this book
for your inspection.

Understanding Loss
To Relieve
The Anguish

Then
move ahead

Lloyd E. McIlveen

Order this book online at www.trafford.com
or email orders@trafford.com

Most Trafford titles are also available at major online book retailers.

Print information available on the last page.

ISBN: 978-1-4669-9943-5 (sc)
ISBN: 978-1-4669-9942-8 (e)

Library of Congress Control Number: 2013913719

Trafford rev. 12/03/2015

 www.trafford.com

North America & international
toll-free: 1 888 232 4444 (USA & Canada)
fax: 812 355 4082

The losses I have experienced in my life have far exceeded the gains, but the knowledge I have received from each of those losses could never be taught by the gains per se with all their value.

The educational system is biased for creating gains of which are needed, popular, expensive and in demand. That's the desired view.

There are always plenty of losses of which can't be bought. They are not in demand and the educational value of them has no price. If losses per se have no value, they may not be worth sacrificing one's serenity and dignity during and after a loss. Let's look into it to cut loss feelings down.

L.E.M.

Preface

$\mathcal{G}$aining more of what the experiences of loss amounts to for reducing the unpleasant effects of them is what this book is about even though everyone knows the word loss means something or someone taken away.

The useful value of the term loss is not so much of what is missing, but of what can be gained because of it. What is done is in the past. What can be gained is for the future if and when we can believe we have a future.

When a person hurts from a loss, the strong and normal tendency is either to recover the loss or just get relief from the emotional pain to function in a contented manner once more. That desire for contentment can be a misleading desire without rational perspective of whether the desired feeling will be lasting or not.

An individual can be naturally or educationally intelligent concerning thoughts and ideas, but when a loss suddenly occurs, the emotions aren't usually, naturally and educationally prepared to calmly accept the incident and functions in emotional disarray. This is referred to here as the pain of feelings.

The contents of the following chapters sort out the details of what a person is made up of for contributing toward one's loss or losses, how one reacts with sudden surprises of loss and possibilities of dealing with the misery of loss or offsetting the effects and pain for creative purposes as a result of the loss or losses.

All of the exposure to the nature of human psychology expressed in these texts are intended for purposes of "assisting" in the search for gaining knowledge of how to feel better and possibly resolve or "make up" for losses incurred through being assertively creative. If "cure" of emotional symptoms are acquired, the credit is due to the reader for applying acquired efforts in pursuing that cure. Your author accepts no responsibility of intentions to cure any emotional effects or symptoms. Professional guidance is always recommended where symptoms persist, where confusion exists or where specific questions need to be probed into concerning the emotional effects.

If the reader is serious about reaping the benefits of resolving the effects of loss, taking notes while passing through the chapters and reviewing them will help enhance the resolutions studied.

General speaking, these chapters on understanding loss are author designed for the purpose of helping to reduce emotional pressure associated with shock and grief of losing a job, a title, a career, losing in a marriage, losing certain heritage and rights along with other opportunities, material possessions and even freedom in so many ways, but most of the loss descriptions are focused on losing close relationships through death, anger, court awards, theft and other legal, ricocheting or unduly encounters of which so many times devastates unsuspecting victims or at least irritates, annoys or depresses them.

UNDERSTANDING LOSS TO RELIEVE THE ANGUISH

Contents

Chapter 1

Suffering a loss or not?
That is the question

*H*onesty is always the best policy, like they say, especially when it is dealing with the self. Truth, deception and lies to another person only exist in the quickly fading interim of the self and the other person through the words spoken. Truth, deception and lies, silently or aloud, spoken to the self are a part of the self and will remain part of the self whether they are directed to another person or to the self and will remain within. Those words will become a part of what the self represents and adds toward the formation of the self's character. Deception and lies may not be so helpful when one is dependent on displaying good character to others.

The tendency of displaying feelings of deception to the self can be irresistible. What is the deception? The loss may not amount to something taken away. It may only be a neurotic and selfish feeling of not being more complete in life with a person, health, career or other projects etc. Loss can be something missing inside the self.

Complete honesty to and with the self is needed and required when the self is suffering a loss. When a person is treating others in a selfish and underhanded manner, chances are that person will also suffer complicated and mixed feelings of existence and judgments with that self. The results are favorable the disservice to others will return to the self. That means the adversely developed character and personality of this individual may also suffer unnecessary feelings of guilt which, in turn, can manifest in more emotional suffering such as anxiety of insufficiency, anxiety of nonacceptance and anxiety where everything not gained is worse of a loss than being normally honest and truthful concerning the unneeded disservice to the self when these emotional disasters hit. Think about that a little more.

The therapist's and church offices are constantly busy with people who suffer emotional pain because of not understanding how their shifting feelings of loss really work.

Jack was 62 when his wife of 40 years died. Sure, he was upset and became emotionally derailed. He said he would never have another lady again. He didn't want to go through that grief again. Jack, like so many others, didn't know how his feelings worked either. He only suffered that dejected feeling because he didn't understand how one can regulate those feelings. Sure, it's normal to experience sudden feelings of loss, but no one has to suffer so bad as to give up or descend into an emotional turmoil and that doesn't mean we have to continue reacting in that particularly "normal" fashion because of a loss and go down the tube emotionally.

Gaining and losing is a way of life; some more and some less. It's better to be prepared for the possibility of having more losses because fairness is not guaranteed in this life on planet Earth anymore than it is with the colliding planets and stars in the universe.

Jack rejected the notion of having those wonderful feelings with a mate again based on fear the possible loss would or might create another loss and more bad feelings. He reacted in that manner because of his insufficient programming to handle loss. He was programmed with scattered principles, ideas and beliefs as so many have. For instance, he was conventionally religious and thought he would be with his wife after death in heaven. He contradicted himself. If they were to meet in heaven, his fretting would be unnecessary because of believing heaven existed. Jack's system of believing was unsupportive and left him a victim of emotional loss. So many people do this. Some catch on and make changes and others get lost in their confusion with their mixed ideals. More on this ahead.

No one has to immeasurably suffer from loss in particularly when they can avoid it. The conventional concept of loss can be a prerequisite for a gain of something else or maybe even of the same nature or better. It's all in how one chooses to approach the matter mostly based on programming of belief from the past. That can also be changed. Everything "does" change in the universe. Why would our feelings and approaches be any different? Change for the better is better.

The question, right now, is whether a supposed loss is really a loss as is conventionally perceived or is it strictly a weakened state of mind where security is threatened? Sure, all living beings experience what is referred to as strengths and weaknesses. We can nourish those states of mind with "I feel weak" or "I feel strong" and it becomes real and true especially when a person is persistent in believing it or at least help it to unfold one way or another through constant programming, praying and especially believing it however that may be exercised.

Guilt is a driving force that contributes toward "flared up" emotional feelings of remorse when any loss occurs as, "I could have done more," "I didn't have to say those things," "Why wasn't it me," "I could have done it differently," "I deserve this punishment," "I can't believe I did that," "I'm no good," "I'm all washed up now," etc., etc.

Why are people always so sad when encountering a loss? Whatever they had, there is usually more of it in one way or another as far as gaining emotional security is concerned unless they defeatingly and firmly oppose the view of overcoming the misery of their misfortune.

Loss emotions, many times, are justified too firmly by the conventional expectation where one "has" to suffer or not be accepted by others. How about not being accepted even by the self as though it is a traditional and almost inherent instinct? It could be, but we are now smart enough to offset many of our genetic or instinctual tendencies at least to some degrees if not more educationally propagated.

Religious indoctrination and belief can be contradictory at times especially when we see heaven oriented people crying and feeling bad when someone dear passes away. That has a tendency to defeat the belief of after life where the sooner they both die, the sooner they will reunite. That view deserves probing into for more understanding of why and how our dismaying feelings function in any loss.

Even the nonreligious cry and feel bad when death separates them. Why do most of us do it? It has become a cultural instinct that is difficult to resist and almost becomes a must to display and express feelings of loss with slow recovery. The possibility exists where feeling bad is somewhat of a price we must pay for having a comfortable, meaningful, fun or joyous experience with someone or something previous to the occurrence of the loss.

True, when one is grieving, the average person won't ask why because grieving isn't a calculable thought and very difficult to make sense out of in the presence of an overwhelming emotional tendency to feel bad. That ensuing grievance appears to be culturally developed in fulfilling its expected destiny and "accepting" the circumstances involved in the so called loss or losses which enslaves the human emotional system almost like we have been educated to do it.

Thought is an ability to decipher, analyze, judge and articulate possibilities where, as opposites unveil, feeling is incapable of directing a course of logical approach to anything except the "lower" states of consciousness as anger, sadness, jealousy, fear, envy and the like. That may be good reason why people grieve so miserably other than just feeling bad. They are hovering in a lower state of consciousness and are very vulnerable to victimization of themselves as well as from opportunists who intellectually as well as emotionally "feed" on these emotionally seized individuals who have allowed themselves to be magnetized into this state. This can be viewed as a self-inflicted disease of sadness and misery. That state of mind isn't necessary or required for living our lives with losses. We don't need emotional "traps" we have allowed ourselves to trip into just because it seems the "thing to do."

The process of grieving from this so called loss can be relearned with awareness that loss is only a psychological perception of leaving something behind or having it taken away in the sense that life "does" continue way into the future and loss is a natural part of it for almost everyone.

Whatever is done is done and we "can" regulate our feelings to some degree for what we can believe will be a fitting, necessary, proper, overdue, cultural, religious, surviving or other philosophical manners by utilizing a study of how we began our lives, how we continued through with our lives and what and how we now choose to be, think and feel. The key to this success is adapting to more of our choices to be utilized.

Yes, it does require some searching, new programming and letting some of that old programming fall to the wayside that isn't helping our cause. The exception is when a person chooses to be masochistic, a martyr or inflexible with the enhancing values of change.

Being fired, abandoned, divorced, discredited or making a terrible mistake etc. are all ego disturbing sensations and are subjects of experiencing descending spirit of which, in this case, is a degraded feeling of loss with no doubt of it.

What we must discern for feeling stronger and less vulnerable with loss of any kind is whether or not indeed we have common and make sense reason to victimize ourselves with immeasurable grievance where loss has suddenly set in. After all, accepting life with all its good things, challenges, shams and disappointments alike; isn't loss just a part of it in its overall development?

Whether a loss needs to be a heart stabbing misery that causes one's life to emotionally derail and become unstable or whether that reaction to loss is much less emotional and only a small reality is the ongoing question here and forward. Let's look at it.

Symptoms of our culturally influenced miseries accompanying losses appear necessary to prevent guilt feelings or indifference when slapped with that sudden realization of the loss.

The more we learn about how necessary or not it is to constantly nourish these tormenting feelings of loss, the easier and faster the symptoms of loss will fade. Stay aware of that more often.

After all, we humans don't always have complete control of our reactionary feelings when sudden surprises occur and let's face it, feeling emotionally miserable doesn't really serve any worthwhile cause except maybe to teach us more how to not be miserable

However and whatever feelings of loss may be, they can all be reduced significantly and meaningfully with a little or more probing. Give it a whirl. Why suffer? Let's build some confidence in "this" area.

Chapter 2

How did the loss begin?

$\mathcal{W}$hen a loss occurs, whoever thinks or analyzes where, when and how it began? When it does occur, logic takes a back seat and emotions tend to lead the way which usually slows down any needed progress of offsetting or correcting the reactionary condition of loss and makes one feel worse than may be necessary.

So, if one with enough educational background or sufficient desire chooses to emancipate that feeling of loss to rationally correct, compensate or make creative adjustments to it, that person will look into the mind and books for enough information concerning the chronological events; even psychological attributions that add toward the ill and painful experience of depressed feelings from loss. Almost all depression arises from something lost or from something not gained among past rearing or mental disenchantment.

Loss apparition and/or phobia can originate at a very young age and cause life long depression and supports the dreary feelings of losing anything. Psychotherapy has been known to releave some of the effects related to depression and the losses agitated by it. Many of us have depression subdued or controlled.

The experience of any emotionally felt loss isn't always a feeling that happens on the spot. It is a feeling as a result of insufficient preparation. The actual loss isn't nearly as significant as the feeling of being miserable because of it. When one is in dire pain, escaping that pain is highest on the list of priorities, right? The actual loss doesn't experience pain. It's over and done. The griever is left with the painful effects.

The loss "begins" near the spot, but those feelings of the loss only "erupt" when the emotional system of mind was developing and maturing with family, friends and from various sources of exploitation and indoctrination. Did any of them ever teach how to avoid emotional pain from losses? Probably not too many, if any. If they did, the recipients probably didn't practice much of it. Everything learned must be practiced regularly to some degree. More practice yields better results. That practice allows us less vulnerability to loss illness.

Many dignitaries and other leaders in prominent positions have, in their own ways, been psychologically prepared for family deaths, kingdom or ruler takeovers, cataclysmic disasters of earthquakes, hurricanes, floods, fires and somehow managed to remain reasonably calm. They established a strict posture to remain emotionally invulnerable. They were guided to become and stay aware of being that person of emotional stability. Occasionally, their losses were great, but their emotional reactions weren't as devastating as the average unguided individual. Jackie Kennedy was one of those grand examples of emotional and physical stability especially during the long ordeal at her husband's funeral back in the sixties.

Stanley was raised by wonderful, loving parents and sisters. They all lived and worked on an exciting thoroughbred horse ranch. They all loved the life of raising racehorses and were inseparable. They knew horses and racing inside and out. They knew and appreciated the value of family camaraderie with friends and workers.

All was well until Stanley's wife became ill and died. The remainders of the family were, indeed, devastated and lost incentive to pursue their careers. Time passed and expenses were devouring their capital along with no derby wins. Their best horse broke a leg. Everything seemed to be tumbling and deteriorating.

They were all fairly well prepared for good family repour, love, respect and compatibility, but they weren't prepared for family loss which, so much of the time, strikes suddenly when one least expects it to happen.

Where did it begin? Was it with the decision to start a family? Maybe it was the decision to raise horses. Maybe the blame can simply be attributed to the death of Stanley's wife or maybe because of a fantasy where nothing bad could ever happen to them? We might be getting close.

Most things considered, the family had a pretty good thing going in their domestic venture. When they started the business, all appeared glorious and rewarding. They were optimistic, ambitious and like so many people, didn't prepare for any personal disasters. That may have contributed to their vulnerability of being emotionally shocked.

Let it be known to all who may be unaware, ignorant, naive or embossed in an embedment of pure fantasy, extreme loss of this nature is certainly nothing new and is degrading and depressing to the very core of one's family existence which causes some to break ties and venture out in their separate directions while others cling to one another.

The good news is these incidents of emotional instability "can" be prevented from deteriorating by, again, looking at creative possibilities. Some may say preparing for worse scenario possibilities is negative thinking and may "cause" adverse problems. If that's the case, the fire department might just as well not have strict laws and rules for preventing fires and the water dams of the world might as well not have control dampers. How about stopping the use of pesticides for preventing pest infestation? The longer the world turns, the more need there is for preventive methods. This is an example for preventing the sickening feelings of loss remorse and sorrow of which taxes one's health, contentment and existence.

We have been entering more into a world of preventive methods in almost every walk of life. It works. Preventing emotional derailment is no exception. It is needed now more that ever. Let's be as realistic as we can be.

The bottom line of resolving many problems of emotional, domestic, romantic, business, national and international nature lies in probing into what and how they all began, sorting them out and little by little agreeing on preventing methods "before" any further steps of progress are initiated. This probing is needed and "is" educational for offsetting needless sorrows.

We are proving preventive methods work well. They are here to stay and must not be viewed as negative programming. Preventing is to save for improved progress. Besides, the tip of an arrow is considered to go forward (positive) and the tail follows (negative or the other end). Electricity moves forward from a source (positive) and returns back to the source (negative). They exist one with the other in all cases of classical or quantum physics. The term negative has been recently expressed in social conversation in an illogical fashion. All they are really saying is, "Don't do it your way. Do it my way." It's a biased accusation to say, "Don't be negative." A negative route is not an opinion of right, wrong, should or shouldn't. It's simply the opposite of positive or the end; not good, fitting or bad in any sense.

There was a herd of 100 antelopes when the lion attacked one of them. Now the herd has a negative antelope in that herd. That isn't an opinion or an accusation. It's just what negative is. It's also a human version of nonacceptance.

What does positive and negative have to do with how loss began? Plenty. Understanding loss better helps to relieve the pain of which hasn't been understood by so many for millennium's of time. Knowing whether the suffering is positive or negative can help rearrange invalid or sorrowful feelings, so it must not be misunderstood wherever possible.

The bad feeling is generally assumed to be a negative feeling because it's unpleasant and those kind of feelings are opposite to pleasant feelings. Negativeness is opposition or side effects of or to an object or opinion. Most everyone doesn't really want to be considered opposite or on another end of things moving forward, right? A reasonable alternative is to join the positive movement forward in the mind. Make a declaration to move into front seat thinking which is leading the chosen way, not back seat thinking which is being pulled or trailing. That may help alienate a lot of the opposition contentions concerning opposition "attitude."

This subject of positive/negative will probably remain a subject of debate for some time to come because of "its" differences on how it can be viewed and applied. We really do have the right to view it all in any way for allowing us to counteract sorrow feelings. A spaceship's exhaust (negative) moves in the opposite direction of its forward movement (positive). Think.

When people realize how and when their present state of making constant decisions and experiencing emotional reactions began and developed, it will be a time to redirect them by reprogramming the psyche of thoughts and feelings for the benefit of learning and practicing either "new" or "other" methods to focus and stay on them. Those courses will be to maintain and regulate emotional reactions for continuously changing gains and losses which will be a way of life in emotional stability. Handling life is a constant series of gains and losses. We must be aware that is how everything started with mankind and isn't much different now. We must see it as "just" gains and losses for our survival of contentment, not good and bad. Good is okay, but bad doesn't conventionally seem to have much value even though it's integrally a part of it all.

This emotional stability in relationship with the reaction of loss is acquired through the knowledge of how those reactions were first noticed, if and when they continued and what the feelings of confidence, optimism or fear existed each time. The time looking into it will be well worth it.

The future is right for regulating feelings. Viewing future as plenty of time in comparison to not enough time allows us the calm and collected rationale of realizing we don't have to follow suit of ancient history where people have wastefully and uncreatively suffered feelings of loss.

What we want to avoid, in preventing loss misery, is what appears to be a strong human tendency to repeat habits over and over. If those habits are well directed for specific reasons which will be a benefit to the individual and possibly others along with that individual, all may be well.

However, if one is unaware those habits are adding toward emotional instability, those habits will continue forming one's platform of contention which may not be conducive to one's emotional contentment. This study may raise one's awareness of that possibility and one will have the chance to change that quagmire that inhibits emotional strength and comfort.

When one acquires these "new" states of mind awareness, gathering knowledge in perspective of how the excruciating feelings of loss or disappointments began and continued will draw a clearer picture for understanding and incrementally gaining that calmer stability of mind we refer to as "being cool" or more emotionally stable.

Chapter 3

Is it a new experience or "old hat?"

*M*arion has had some bad luck or was it luck at all? She was successful in her career as a fine actress. She made a lot of money and acquired many friends, she thought. However, she began to realize, after awhile, she didn't really have "meaningful" friends who cared enough to be around her just because they liked her. They just wanted to adhere to her successes, money, parties and the social flair of which tended to open new doors for more of the same.

Marion became somewhat nauseated with the whole scene and was advised to see a therapist to help understand why she felt so uncomfortable. She made an appointment and discovered her phony mannerisms as an actress were rubbing off onto her friends and they, in turn, were treating her the same way she treating them.

Marion had lost her natural character and was reacting with an experience where she so much became the acting part characters and noticed it seemed mysterious, annoying and wouldn't go away.

Time passed and slowly she weaned herself away from acting because her character became habitually repetitive to the tune of being "old hat" and difficult to change. She was getting back what she "put out." She knew she had to make some changes that would separate her from that life of displaying a pretentious facade of herself.

After some insightful changes in completing her acting contracts, she acquired another profession of a clothes designer while developing a more meaningful character within and a new host of caring friends.

Marion's emotional system responded with much more control over her new career's objectives and less emotional disappointments in her perception of losses.

"Old hat" experiences or habits of which are not rewarding can be pretty annoying and even boring when they become what seems unbendable, unbreakable or stagnant. That's when experiences can be referred to as old hat, like they say. New experiences are needed to break the trend of the old hat type. That's healthy and those new "emotional" health habits prevent breakdown when the reaction to loss occurs. Sports men and women know this to be true. Competitive sports is all about winning "and" losing. They must think optimistically and at the same time be prepared to realistically and unpretentiously accept the rather perplexing reality of not winning "after" it happens. That frame of mind helps maintain an uncrumbling stability of emotions. It's not ridding ourselves of emotions. It's just improving and developing them for more stability and less vulnerability to "breaking down."

Life is full of unexpected surprises as we know. Looking forward to "any" possibilities must not be considered as worrying or negative thinking. Welcoming possibilities is maintaining awareness, for instance, that competition and sharing are healthy for everyone; in different degrees of course. Whether those activities are in a class of math, at the ballpark, a business, employment, having most friends in a card game or whatever else, it's all what keeps life moving and "alive!" Even wars, as degrading as they have seemed, have brought about tremendous advances and improvements of adding toward better and longer life so we may learn more on how to survive and manage our many new experiences requiring firm, flexible and stable emotions when the going gets a little or more rough.

The possible wonders, glories and/or difficulties after death cannot be coherently or intelligently agreed upon to surmise the actuality or nature of them by mortalistic evaluation, so we might as well adapt ourselves to the process of probing into and improving our abilities to deal more efficiently, calmly and compatibly with our affairs while we are living. We must refrain from speculating and living our lives around how, where, when and under what circumstances we will die. That's influential programming and can contribute toward an earlier death than figured. It may be considered cheating oneself of life.

Part of life is about reminiscing and learning from ancient, interim and recent experiences in a fashion, beneficially that is, so they will add toward resilient and even exuberant realizations. Those realizations will allow us to become the natural beneficiaries of expanded knowledge, adaptability to change and subjects of which retains a position of comfortable and stable emotions. This is what we are working on to make loss seem less agonizing.

The experiences of too many relatives or friends dying, loved ones leaving home, thefts, job losses, poor investments, surgical failure or hair losses etc, can cause stress and fatigue among other dismaying pressures to the point of "What next?" or "I can't handle this." Allowing that emotional pressure to build up can result in anywhere from a couple of tears to a lengthily session of weeping aside from a hysterical outburst of uncontrolled emotions; even possible suicide to say nothing of heartbreak or hostility toward others as a result. Yes, one thing can lead to another where losses hit or hover unchecked in the minds of humans. Tis a shame because it can all be prevented by proper training from parents, teachers, friends, relatives, seminars, doctors or anyone who is aware (even the self) of how formed habits can jeopardize or favor one's emotions when the chips are down. The contents of this book will also be a link in the improvement of emotional stability. As always, repeat study enhances the multiplicity of knowledge in this area as in so many others.

"Old hat" is also routines we were taught from childhood such as expectations and feeling ashamed because of not agreeing or being constantly ridiculed and accused of being stupid or in the way etc.

Similarities happen even to well adjusted people years later too. Adding them all together forms ongoing pressure within and frustrating emotional reaction especially when one has no knowledge of why because of being preoccupied with so many other desires, activities and ambitions etc.

One can become a wasted victim of one's own programmed past or through knowledge acquired from that past. One can also change those reactions from caring, logical and stable reaction to the appearance of loss. Eventually, the word loss won't be conceived as, "My whole world is crushing" or "I can't handle this." The loss will exist as a base for exercising abilities to be creative with new insight, plans and development. The so called losses will be absorbed in stride and viewed as part in the stages of life and not as something terrible, devastating or unmanageable.

Acquired emotional development can unfold from studying and practicing the material in these chapters.

Experiences of any nature can always be viewed as opportunities for creating, recreating, altering, correcting or making definite changes and not be stuck in "old hat" situations. Breaking old habits for new ones whenever and wherever possible is what helps in acquiring that emotional development.

The "old hat" concept where repetitiously proven acts of wisdom certainly must not be ignored and set off to the side as merely a relic of ancient thinking. Some of the ancient ideas, beliefs, cultural basis and civil philosophies etc. are still very much relied upon in backward and progressively maturing societies. Just remember, though, all of those mentioned virtues are only basics at a time and must not be viewed as rigid barriers restricting uninhibited growth of perception and perspective.

The universe and "all" in it is a conglomeration of progressively gaining, losing and changing phenomena throughout. Why would we be any different. Do we think we are exceptions? Can we defy the influences and natural forces of nature and all its history?

"Old hat" may suffice for old, withered and terminal thinking, but even that can be rearranged as long as one can say. "Yes, let's do it. I want to feel and be more stable with myself and others as a committed desire and duty."

What we all want is good basis of health, confidence and security of stable emotions. That "is" what allows us to cope much easier with loss of any kind. When this is accomplished, let us stay focused on maintaining and believing in this way of life for continued comfort of mind.

While breaking these old habits, one must be sure to assertively gain beneficially new ones quickly so one won't have the tendency to continue with the old ones or revert back to the old habits as time passes. Purposely practicing the new ones must be engaged in a serious manner or that habit reversion may creep back unnoticed and one may think it's not possible to effectively reprogram new ways.

Perseverance and belief in the cause will promote that reprogramming.

"Old hat" concepts, actions, habits and the results of them are, in one way or another, what causes inflexibility. Inflexibility causes stagnation and prevents stimulating growth which is what healthy aliveness is about. Health aliveness automatically supports strength and youthful motivation for stability in all respects of plants, animals, insects and humans.

New or "different" hats are always needed to prevent the "sad sack" image of vulnerable characteristics in people who repeat what seems like unbreakable traditions of succumbing to tendencies of emotionally breaking down when appearances of so thought of "loss" occurs.

This publication on "Understanding Loss To Relieve The Anguish" may seem a bit or more cold natured and possibly a subject of exploiting the mind to turn off feelings as indicated elsewhere in this book, but the intention is not to "numb" the mind. The intention is to clear the mind of traditional and "old" exploitation of which has inhibited people from emotionally and effectively dealing with reality that we deserve.

Clearing the mind of the old inhibitions is where this term "old hat" originated. Old hat pertaining to loss is really a waste of energy. We only have so much of that in this life. Let's string it out for a longer and more rewarding life ahead by exchanging or blending in with newly and rearranged emotions for creative endeavors, not boring ones from the dead past. Sound cruel or cold?

Seems pretty cruel and cold to the self in responding to loss with upset, torturous and ill feelings especially when carried too far after the incident of loss happened and was pretty much over. Let's learn how to release loss.

There is so much stability of mind available for staving off the misery of pain from loss. Why not go for a trip in this area of mind control and experience its reliability?

Chapter 4

One loss "can" lead to another

$\mathcal{B}$e aware of it so it can be prevented. Actually, what can be more unintelligent and frustrating than making the same mistakes on a constant bases? Well, even brilliant people do it sometimes. Of course, that word constant does have its limits and variations with different people.

Loss, being something taken away, something squandered, something abused or something ignored has its magnetism toward repeating its performance. This doesn't pertain to loss of life. It only pertains to individuals who suffered loss in relationships of material possessions or position in life etc. from repeated and unfavorable habits as was similarly mentioned in the last chapter.

When most people enter a building to attend a meeting (church, a dance, a cocktail lounge), they sit in their usual seats which is strictly habitual and are examples of the tendency to repeat in almost everything they do including, without being consciously being aware of it, their programmed actions to lose something or "lose out" on an opportunity. The old expression "you can't win" is a typical set up for creating loss because the one who states it believes it; hence, it becomes true and real. Another expression of loss is "That's the story of my life," which if it concerns loss, is programming for further loss. How about, "I never do anything right," or "Why is it always me?" All those thoughts are manners of maintaining vulnerable consciousness and activates the actuality of it happening again. Paradoxically, this can be referred to as negative thinking causing a positive action as follows:

The positive repeat action is where

"You can't win" becomes "You won't win."

"That's the story of my life" becomes "That's still my life."

"I never do anything right" becomes "I'm not doing anything right."

"Why is it always me?" becomes "It's still me."

So, these negative conscious statements and their reactions taxes one's energies ever so needed especially when suffering emotional dismay of a death, divorce, stock market crash or similar disappointments.

Repetition is great for gaining knowledge, meaningful friends and move creatively forward, but not so good when overemphasized thoughts and feelings are added toward the depression and energy draining mind-set of severe loss.

Dwelling on anything tends to "feed" the growth of the thought. Dwelling on the death of a loved one has possibilities of arousing or continuing repetitious cycles of loss mentality at the time and certainly won't bring back the person or whatever else appears final in the loss. Finality of loss can be accepted or denied. If it is accepted, that frame of mind will be nourished with a certain growth of confidence into a new area of creativity (a little different with each person). That nourishment will be received from various sources depending on how one believes and the strength of their beliefs and choices. There again, if the finality of loss is denied or ignored, the process of emotional "and" mental stability can be hampered, delayed and can also deteriorate. That's important to keep in mind.

The reader, by now, may get the idea, "This is just a lot of talk, but what do I do about it to make my feelings stop hurting?" Rest assured, gaining as much awareness as possible concerning what has happened in the past while gaining more awareness of possibilities, factors, experiences and reactions etc. of what loss is all about and what their reactions can be will enhance a broader perspective as time passes, thereby enabling the reader to exercise those unfortunate and ill contaminated feelings to a point of making changes somewhat automatically with the nourishment of new realizations. Continue these studies. They will help with your present ills.

Since one thing does usually lead to another, we must educate ourselves ahead of time as a prerequisite and well programmed emotional system for any surprise incidents of emotional taxation.

One can never do too much in preparing for the possibility of change, making changes and flowing compatibly with those changes.

This change making perspective is a growth development and as any other growth development, it requires continuity, persistence, belief processing and patience. The combination almost always works quite well in producing desirable results for handling loss without unwanted suffering. Just being aware of repeat patterns having caused much emotional dismay is beneficial in adding toward new goals of emotional improvement and confidence. It's all educational and that, once more, is what is needed.

Certain repetitious patterns of presenting oneself to oneself and others can also lead one astray from self-improvement and interrelation objectives with a pessimistic and higher than thou know it all attitude, so be careful. The other side of that coin of repetitious patterns state one can attract self-improvement and meaningful relationships by gaining a wider scoped and humble self-presentation due to having acquired and improved emotional control. It all adds up.

Under the heading of preventive methods, exercising emotional control with the self while alone and in the presence of others will be a plus in the prevention of what can be stated as unnecessary and emotional outbursts, embarrassment, indignity and show of frailty. We must practice being mentally, emotionally and physically strong for resistance to that well mentioned loss vulnerability.

We can all let our emotional reactions run loosely to-and-fro in however they were inherited, influenced or programmed from the past and either enjoy the fortunately good results or pay the price (however that may be) of traditionally influenced averages where loss reactions have existed with painful reminders. Those reminders say, "This is how you are "supposed" to feel and don't resist it!"

Well, you now have the opportunity to largely improve on that old time exercise of misery by realizing it "is" old hat and unnecessary. The old program can be changed and is starting to happen in these scripts. See it that way, adapt to it and it will unfold in exactly the manner and with the effort you approach it.

We can "be" how we think, believe and tell ourselves what we want to be by the use of a planned program which is vocally stated day by day and repetitiously supported as a way of life similar to praying. It can also be thought of "as" praying. Stopping that program may be somewhat or more reverting to the original state of mind similar to not wearing a retainer after having one's teeth straightened.

One loss can lead to another and one gain can lead to another. One of each produces an average. That defeats the purpose of more meaningful value. Stay with a program of gain.

Programming is reminded in different manners throughout these chapters.

Anything pertaining to belief and its potentials, strengths and usefulness can be viewed in other books written by your author which are listed in the back of this book.

The value of this chapter's concept of one loss leading to another indicates directing and controlling emotional chaos in loss can build stamina and resistance to a vulnerability of which may accompany too many adverse allowed reactions to losses occurring. Stay focused on what these chapters are saying for a much better future. Losses of "some" natures may linger longer; especially if not handled wisely.

Chapter 5

A glutton for punishment or just an education?

$\mathcal{B}$ursting and extended sorrowful feelings when life's possessions or experiences have taken a reverse direction can certainly be viewed as a cultural, traditional and/or emotional reaction and does vary from one person to another. However and after a reasonable period of time has passed, continuous fretting over what has possibly been an inevitable or self-instigated and reversed situation commonly called loss, the fretting may have taken over the individual's spirit and will to work the many opportunities still available. Those opportunities can be equally if not more rewarding as some of the past experiences. It "is" their decision to "do" something about it other than remain with the existing habitual state of mind. That state of mind "can" be directed out of mind.

Some, if not many conventionally religious beliefs profess death is reason for the living to be joyous and celebrate because it's a step toward heaven. Most of the world's people claim being conventionally religious, but happiness doesn't seem to dominate in the death scene at funerals or afterward. If one is truly and conventionally religious, once again, wouldn't it seem logical or fair to practice the seemingly accepted ideas, beliefs and rules etc. of celebrating death instead of mourning, sometimes giving up and not following their established religious ways, mannerisms and guidelines?

Those assumed contradictions of conformity display appearances where reaction feelings have little, if no, relativity to or with the divine manner of belief.

Those who do "not" practice divine belief also mourn in a similar fashion and weep, fret and attend funerals with a similar respect as the religious people do. The real, living value of funerals and fretting is where it brings people together for meaningful sharing, communicating and respect. That is all about "living," not dying. Sometimes it's about accepting and moving forward, not stagnating or giving up at "any" age, circumstance or position. So many of the one's closest to the deceased experience the shocks and after shocks related to deaths and are unprepared to "weather the storm" of victim emotions. That's where this study can help.

The loss of material things, romance, health position in society or just life is still a "going without" or "not having" state of mind. When one doesn't have whatever was lost, it still hurts as is commonly thought of, but is much better emotionally separated in the mind as something that can be compensated for in one form or another. After all, in view of the last few paragraphs, most people seem to agree death is final and life as we understand it cannot be retrieved. However, with those of us who are "alive," everything has a possibility of reappearing in some way or another. That's where these suddenly appearing losses "can" be viewed only as making a change and not like a disaster happening.

Therefore and with all living beings and things, everything is available to have and do which includes not beating our heads against the wall overexercising our habitual tendencies, genetic or developed, to strain our energies with wasteful, exuberant, exhausting and depressed states of mind whenever there is a severe loss.

The question here is what is more important in this life; having things and people etc. or maintaining a good feeling? People and things come and go in this life and there is no reason, other than eccentric and self-defeatism, for us to victimize or punish ourselves just to acquire an education on how to feel bad. Let's utilize the education to feel good and better.

Sure, we may feel emotions of being stripped somehow, maybe robbed, denied, incomplete, defeated or various types of loneliness among other sad feelings. However, we don't need to continue saturating ourselves in knee deep sorrow as though it's going out of style. That's near masochistic self-indulgence and one must not allow that torture. Understanding function of loss helps damper the disappointments and sadness.

If we discovered we had to suffer grief all our lives, we might decide to exchange things and people for just feeling good. There is nothing quite like it; feeling good that is. That's what we are all learning here and that includes your author. When we learn to feel good about ourselves, we are better for others.

Luckily or skillfully, we who are still living have our choice of how to maintain our state of mind and body while we are here on Earth regardless of what may appear lost. Usually, after all is said and done, the most necessary attribute toward living a lengthily and contented life is mental, emotional and physical stability such as feeling steadily good is. If and when we choose that way of life, everyday decisions will hinge on methods, in this case, for preventing emotional suffering from steady symptoms of grief due to loss of any kind.

The stronger and more habitual tendency to justify and continue feelings of grief, regardless of a loss in a death, a job, a romance or a diamond ring etc., can be motivated and perpetuated by saying, thinking or somehow proclaiming, "I'll never get over it unless I commit myself to feeling bad in exchange for my ignorance and wrong doings." That suggestion, "I'll never get over it" is effective and profound programming and will add toward its ongoing effects. Eliminating those negative statements silently or aloud and reprogramming them will turn the negative thinking around with, for instance, "I only allow thoughts in my head which are emotionally, socially, spiritually and objectively creative and useful for the purpose of compatibly adapting with my environment in an acceptably stable manner." Another helpful program can be, "I will train my emotional responses to maintain composure and stability so I can manage my affairs more objectively than by loose and incoherently oriented response."

The preceding suggestions are only examples. Hopefully, the reader will get the general idea for making programming statements of which will influence and change the process of thinking and becoming what that reader chooses to be as time passes. Then follow through by practicing whatever program is accepted or devised on a regular bases day by day with that passage of time or until those suggestions become an inherent part of the subconscious mind to where one can depend on feeling the confidence and stability expected of that approach. One has the choice to regulate that programming accordingly.

Changing one's ways usually resolves most problems and griefs, but does require a decision to do it and utilize determination based on either fear of penalty, desire to improve or simply to survive in self-comfort the best way one knows how at the time.

This chapter is indicative of a choice more than a tendency to regulate one's feelings. Many therapists profess feelings have a mind of their own and are difficult to change. That is calculated theory and is not particularly contested here, but guess who that mind belongs to. Right, the self. The self "owns" that mind of it's own and therefore "can" be regulated through reasoning, analyzing and reprogramming the conscious thoughts into the subconscious mind for storage and use when chosen.

Why be a self-chosen or influenced glutton for punishment? There are so many things in this life that can be lost, misplaced, stolen, illegally snatched or used, mistaken, confiscated, misdirected, misunderstood and a longer list of personal and material surprises that can leave one feeling negative, down and near out, depressed and even victimized. If it makes sense to offset and/or change those reactions for better and ongoing resistance to grief, then educational guidance toward regulating the control and symptoms of grief will fittingly serve a most beneficial cause.

Regulating our emotional reactions to grief of loss won't leave us helplessly immune or insensitive to and with human sensations, feelings or other sensitive people; not at all. It will serve us and others as a good representative of acquired stability. If we choose, we will still have the inborn ability to be sentimental or cry whenever we "allow" or "let" it happen. Having stable emotions doesn't stamp out our ability to experience natural urges of which our bodies and minds were designed for, if you will. We only need to regulate the overuse of boisterous, undignified or excess emotions do to feelings of loss and their relativities.

The process of searching, discovering, developing and programming for handling grief will be an advantage for developing new, needed, lasting perspective and strengths to blend with and tackle future encounters of grief due to loss in a more secure and balanced manner. It works.

Sincere, assertive and determined efforts to understand loss more clearly is of the essence in overcoming excessive emotional pain and anxiety caused by loss.

Through these studies, one can learn to understand more clearly, other than what one already knows, how loss can be viewed and how easily or traumatically the individual feels, can feel or will feel emotionally and physically in the sense of better or worse.

No one cares more than the self how really cool, calm and collected the self can be and it will never be as good as when that person decides to get serious and initiate steady efforts of self-improvements. You've gone this far, now you can win over yourself by continuing these chapters and making amends.

The essence of viewing different aspects of loss for understanding it more lies here in the questions and needs of those who read educational material in this area. They usually amount to # 1, "Will this help fulfill my desire to become what I am shooting for?" # 2, "Can I get a broad perspective on this subject to expand my intellectual perception?" # 3, can be, "Can I learn how to prevent my stomach from getting upset every time I'm thrown off guard by a bad experience?" # 4, also can be, "I thought I had a grip on life and knew it all until I had enough verbal feedback from others telling me I was so mistaken about how people function. Now I need to study more views other than my own how the mind works."

A glutton for punishment syndrome is the type who never studies for improving one's realistic perception and only speaks from guessing and contending how everything and everyone is or functions.

Those who reach out and read specialized material on subjects as how to understand loss, for instance, will gain more useable knowledge on how to not only handle loss better, but also how to relate better on the subject with and to others.

Chapter 6

Dealing with what "seems" the worst in loss

$\mathcal{W}$hen do we determine when a loss is in fact a loss? Jerry collected antiques for many years and finally decided to rent a modest store to collect more antiques and sell others.

He packed a lot of wooden and dry articles in a small area in back of the store. One day there was a fire in the store that burned all his antiques. He was frantically depressed. He lost everything he owned in the fire. Jerry couldn't imagine anything worse than losing everything he had worked for. He became a desolated, dejected and grief stricken victim of unforeseen circumstances. His insurance only covered fire damage on the store. Then he became ill from fretting too much and not doing anything about it. Just another typical case of loss, right? There have been plenty of them and most of the victims eventually manage to recover somehow, but distressingly slow.

Does a person have to suffer from loss several times as an education of preparing for the "big one?" Let's see.

Whether the loss is of a death, a business, a lover, money, dignity or any other meaningful acquirement, the reaction of what seems the worst possibility can either be #1, a feeling of crucial desperation in surrendering all gumption to live and pursue, #2, an objective, but constant emotional pain in taking care of the post loss details much to one's dismay for a certain length of time prior to fully accepting the loss or #3, taken into stride by one who many times may have been trained for sudden traumas and appears insensitive or "cold" in reaction to a loss. Delving into these possibilities with the idea of preparing oneself in preventing them through useful programming or praying can very well trim the suffering aspect when exposed to loss. Remember, it only "seems" to be terrible at the time it happens.

Oh, it's much easier said, but not so easy to do? Well, the first one of those possibilities of desperation is widely experienced and "practiced" many times as a form of martyrizing, but mostly exercised by emotionally sensitive and hysterical proned personalities. The second possibility of constant emotional pain is an average disappointment of surviving mannerism do to pain. These people will do what is immediately necessary along with some of the sympathetic "play acting" they "allow" themselves to engage in especially at funerals and get togethers afterward. The funerals "do" give a person an opportunity to release some of the overwhelming and stored up emotions which is pure reaction with the perception of loss, not the actual object in the loss itself. Theoretically, separating the actual loss from the perception and studying it for awhile can be very helpful in reducing emotional pain as mentioned. Stay focused on separating them. #3, the worst possible reactions is either a developed reaction of emotional control or a "toughened in" attitude of protection against emotional breakdown usually resulting from too many losses incurred over a period of time. If that's the case, it may be time to acquire a little more wisdom or get "toughened." How about both?

Loss reaction varies from one person to the next. Loss reaction mannerisms can be genetically and/ or instinctually inclined particularly in younger people who, in most cases, haven't experienced multiple counted losses, natural disasters, genocide conditions or extended time in areas of war as examples.

Severe loss reaction mannerisms of overprotected, very sensitive and vulnerable personalities can be triggered by sheer fear of feeling shakey and adversely insecure during or shortly after the time of experiencing the loss.

Other cases of the "toughened in" attitude include an objective view where one is lucky enough to be "trained" for managing emotional control for the benefit of preventing a domino effect of "losing" control of one's composure, dignity, temperament and emotional dexterity.

Since life sometimes seem cluttered with what may appear undue, disturbing and disappointing surprises, it would behoove one to study and practice or be trained in this process of offsetting erratic and unnecessary emotional disruption that sometimes becomes influential in that uncontrolled domino effect of loss reaction. Emotional therapists can help.

Dealing with the worst scenario is only a describable and technical state of mind! That is, when a person "believes" the worst is happening or can happen, it may truly "seem" the worst. What "seems" to be is only an approximate view. The strength of viewpoint is more in what is believed. Belief in words and feelings can profoundly accentuate and manifest the belief to be true. "That" truth may be a deception to the self and cause the loss reaction to become the "actual" worst that can happen and not the loss itself. It's tricky. Watch it!

The human mind is extensively creative in enhancing one's ability to reap the rewards of "being" creative in pursuing those endeavors. By the same token of creative ability, one can also exercise the negative and energy draining route of accomplishment by developing adverse, destructive and detrimental affects to the common cause of survival and contentment by viewing, initiating and supporting worse scenarios and their possibilities.

The human mind "does" have capabilities of flexing and changing the state of thinking and feeling for a happier, contented and compatible attitude on life "or" for a masochistic and set mannerism of attracting painful situations including the disturbing magnetism of loss and sorrow because of it. That magnetism has appearances of, like they say, a fire waiting to happen.

The example of defeat in that paragraph is typical of a mindset, engraving or implant of adversely narrow and fanatically influenced ideals from parents, teachers or other exploitive sources. Those influences can hang on for many years and "can" be broken down for more creative and rewarding purposes. Look for them and make corrections.

The worst in losses isn't limited to just losses as in the worst that can happen probably will. This manner of "believing," per se, is also utilized by anyone untrained, by trained belief from others who have been trained with limited, narrow or adverse belief or from a choice pursued by virtue of a broadly scoped mentality. Belief, however interpreted, is what makes anything go, stand still or stop. It's all powerful and open for anyone in any way. Choose carefully.

Those who resist change are harnessed with anxiety and remain narrow, inhibited and set. Change and redevelopment through many other means usually results in a more robustly, healthy, exciting, contented and more relaxed manner of living, relating and coexisting. This is what is needed with losses.

Dealing with the ups and worst downs of loss is challenging and when they are present, they take the boredom out of life. The fact is, the terribleness mindset of loss is never as bad as it is emotionally surmised and perceived and it "is" alterable.

Sometimes our very human imaginations "stretch" losses out to be more excessive and even to the point of being extravagant when they can actually be contained. There is an old saying that indicates things have a way of working themselves out. Your author says, once again, it only "seems" bad at the time it happens.

A little study, patience and positive belief will, as always, reduce what "seems" to be a grieving feeling. Looking at the grievance and even analyzing what it is will lessen the effects sooner, especially with that belief.

However the belief is utilized in an optimistic approach for reducing the effects of loss misery, it "is" an inward and personal battle. One must not perceive it as something where one believes the problem will go away "only" by understanding it more. Here's why:

The state of thinking where the loss only "seems" the worst in its nature can be a powerful feeling which may reduce the anxiety in emotional suffering. Be aware, though, that may be an illusive thought in assuming the battle is over.

Most battles do not conclude by sheer understanding. They are "won" through understanding, careful planning, substantial strategy for approach, determination and a positive and forward commitment to win.

Winning over our self-made anxieties that causes emotional pain has similar requirements. Without accepting them, the results of reducing loss effects may be mediocre. The strongest desire to win usually does. This is where that very powerful factor of choice and decision runs the show to start the battle, if you will. Touche to and with the self.

Winning this battle with the self is all reasonably accomplishable. At least there is no outside the self competition to give you a hard time. Your success of obtaining calm can be shared with others and that can be an appreciated endeavor. That can also be a confidence booster and if constantly practiced, can be a very rewarding lifestyle of emotional strength and stability.

Chapter 7

Dealing with achievements in loss

*A*chievements are similar to acquirements. They have no specific value until a descriptive and qualifying adjective is placed before them as "meaningful," "technical" or "brilliant" for instance. Achievement in loss has to be "boiled down" to an opinion, a biased or even prejudicial viewpoint or a telltale description which expresses the value of the achievement. One might say it's good and another might say it's not good and so forth. This is an important reminder of what may seem a meaningful achievement to one may seem a much less or even apposite value to another. That's where the value of patience, understanding and a reasonably tolerable state of mind comes in pretty handy where people dealing in loss is concerned.

Two views of loss in the previous chapter dealt with the objects or persons taken away and their traumatic reactions. What more is there?

A third very real, but not so conventionally accepted alternative to or with the normally creative view of achieving in loss is to avoid ongoing traumas of loss by shutting off the mind or running away from it all, so to speak which is not so good. This is done, of course, with the use of alcohol, drugs, being super busy, overeating, overindulging in other inhibitors of normal progress and avoiding creative change.

The other and more conventionally optimistic view of the third alternative is to utilize the inevitable or sudden reaction of loss to help heal the sickened emotions, resolve adversities of them and move on with the business of life's progress without a dragging tail of heavy, emotionally impeding hindrances to what may be considered normal contentment.

Sure, it "seems" a difficult time when loss occurs. However, overindulgence in allowing that difficulty to dominate can be somewhat or more avoided by a little study and acquired awareness in the beginning course of the loss. Let's continue the course of gaining loss awareness to prevent its misery.

The running away or avoidance syndrome of mind is one's excessively fearful and characteristical disposition. So many cases involve being impervious to receiving help even "or" especially with the experience of a qualified therapist in this area of psychodynamics. This runaway or avoidance syndrome is many times referred to as a state of denial as many of you may already know.

So, other than the choice of avoidance or denial that usually takes a much longer time to resolve in the effects of loss or any other emotional inhibitors, what is left in the pursuit of the third view other than being unconventionally stubborn and resistant to compatible relating and/or expressing misery of loss?

First, in the normally creative view of accomplishments in loss, we possess a willingness based on a desire of choice to grow and capitalize on the loss. That means take fair advantage of a loss as an opportunity to create new or even "better" situations than previously existed because, after all, life does move on and we learn from many other or opposite views of loss as well as from the creative aspect.

Both the creative and resisting views of progress in loss may be a disadvantage if utilized as a judgment of good, bad, right or wrong since, as it has been stated, all is fair in love and war; now in the advantages and disadvantages of loss too.

Number two in the third achievement alternatives of loss is to be creative in allowing the headquarters of the conscious mind to lineup the necessary priorities of accomplishment in loss. That has to be an objective approach.

Number three after those priorities is to utilize discipline in forming and maintaining composure even if it means putting on an act; mostly to the self. Stick with the act. There is a more favorable than not possibility of that act becoming a vested habit and virtue toward the prevention of unnecessary grief after any loss or other grievance too.

Number four of the opportunistic priorities is, as mentioned, that which or who was a loss wasn't there before it was owned, borrowed, shared or maintained. In other word's, the loss was only one of the many "experiences" life has been subjected to or will be in the future. It's part of the "scene" of life wherever one may be or pass through. This excessive and irrationally induced reaction to an action of loss is neither required, necessary or even many times meaningful to anyone's cause and only adds toward more of the same dreary facade tendencies. A loss doesn't have to explode bigger than it really is or seems.

Achievements as a result of loss will be duly noticed following the time of grievance with the actual loss along with priority decisions which have been placed in line and steps have been made to proceed with those priorities. This is where one's creativity begins.

Consider these decisions, steps of priorities and promotion of them as a self-creative therapy where proguidance is unavailable. The merits of self "or" professionally guided accomplishment boosts self-esteem and it has a tendency to further perpetuate excitement toward the cause of emotional stability, preventive methods and self-acceptance to say nothing of admiration from others. Doing the work on the mind is great! It helps prevents becoming an emotional victim of sudden depression, loneliness or possible remorseful feelings.

Janice met and fell in love with Greg who engineered and built bridges. They both felt the same way about each other and eventually made plans to get married.

One day, his business group decided to contract a sizable bridge job. Greg would have to go to the middle east for a year of which he did much to

Janice's dismay. She couldn't leave her steady job in the states. Eventually, Greg slowly avoided communicating with Janice. She became frantic with his lack of staying in touch especially when she had a problem getting him on the phone or computer.

Greg had met another woman in the construction office and became deeply involved. Several weeks passed before he e-mailed a letter explaining the job was extended and how he was no longer sure about their proposed marriage.

While the communication was silently lingering, Janice was responding normally as anyone else would under the circumstances. She was upset to the point of being held together with what was compared to weakly woven emotional stitches ready to breach at any moment.

Luckily, Janice had a girlfriend (Norma) who empathized with her emotional turmoil that finally led to outright grief of loss when Greg informed her of his obvious romantic fling. She was hurting and almost in a hysterical rage. This never happened to her. She had never prepared herself for this type of "treatment."

Janice almost violently blamed Greg for a completely unwarranted act of cruelty which is quite typical when hysteria results from relationship turmoil. She also blamed him for becoming sick due to his actions. She experienced a sensation of anger and profound hate of his very existence one moment and a crucial need of the security she had gained with him on the next moment. She was frantic.

Norma somehow convinced Janice to quickly see an emotional therapist. In their meeting, Janice was allowed to screech out her anger and frustration in a safe, but controlled environment. The therapist encouraged Janice to release enough reaction expression and also allowed her to realize when it was going too far. The therapist helped guide Janice through realizations where she didn't "have" to crucify her whole emotional makeup while blaming Greg for "her" sorrow. The therapist also helped Janice to realize by letting Greg be as he is, it also sets her free from any emotional or other connection of him. This is part of the circumstance/ trap syndrome where people are either unknowingly vacuumed into or purposely avoid that trap. Janice could have avoided her misery with prepared efforts of being ready for worse scenario encounters. They hit almost everyone sooner or later. One must always be prepared for circumstantial change. They seem to be on the rise.

Achieving a particular state of mind in any loss becomes a state or frame of mind and is always open for any route one decides to exercise. When one slips into a state of denial, which is the state of refusing any suggestion, the bottom line of who is responsible for that denial lies in the fact the self is doing it to the self and no one else. That person has to get back in line somehow and accept responsibility for any actions or reactions resulting from that unrelenting posture of which can create further psychological insecurities of mind. Unless that person has been proven to be a victim of an uncontrolled mental illness or an award of the court, that self-responsibility further applies and must be accepted to escape defeating traps or circumstantial magnetism. They "can" be avoided with applied insight in being aware of any possibilities.

Normally healthy people can initiate the birthright choice to reshape their grief of loss response so there will be much less misery the next time it happens. Life has many losses and many of us must offset and reduce the misery causing emotions to erupt. Again, it isn't being cold as many would say. It's being stable and stronger for the individual's future. What is lost is done! Let us not dangle on loss. What was lost usually doesn't come back. Let us recover ASAP and move on just as future is inevitably meant to be. Let the lust for achievements continue. There are always more to look forward to. Patience pays with knowledge the "bad" feelings are "only" for the present and can be tapered down or eliminated with the same knowledge we are working on now.

Who thinks of accomplishing anything when they are in the midst of a shock from losing someone or something? Probably not many if any at all. If someone could tell them about their opportunities to creatively prevent repeated miseries while in that state of shock, they probably wouldn't even listen due to their emotional distraction at the time, but there is a chance they may remember what was suggested later. That's when the opportunity has more significance and they may pick up a book on this subject. This is pointed out to emphasize the value of gaining, repeating, believing and practicing knowledge of this nature for maintaining "nerves of comfort" and realizing for every adverse or gloomy appearing incident, there is an opportunity for reducing the painfully emotional effects and recognize the chances to become emotionally "more" stable.

Chapter 8

On the way to rising above adverse reaction to loss

$\mathcal{O}$nce loss has been reasonably accepted as over and done, which may require steady and conscious effort, giant strides can be accomplished in leaving the grief behind. Experiencing loss is partly a state of thinking, but mostly feeling. When that realization is accepted, it's "only" a matter of time for that thinking and feeling to diminish and return to the status quo before the loss. That assurance is something to be optimistic about. If that cannot be accepted, the so-called loss isn't clear at all. Sometimes, one must have more sufficient evidence of it being a loss or maybe an opportunity to take fair advantage of. That pertains to a job, a stolen car, a particular talent, a so-called friend, a love or romance, a chance to be governor or even a fish on the end of a line. Sometimes we grieve over loss and later realize it was only something we became habitually accustomed to and it was just a matter of becoming unaccustomed to. Saying it's psychological is easily said. If we practice the simplicity of this philosophy, that practice and belief will allow the misery of loss to transform into a much easier task to endure. Then, we may discover it wasn't such a loss after all and become relieved and maybe even a little more humble to realize it could have been worse. Some of us may even look at our attitude of loss perception, suspicion or impulsive response of what appears as loss and be willing to indulge in stimulating new knowledge for improvement in that response. It's all available.

Sharon was always self-sufficient and contented by herself. That is, as long as she seemed assured there would be someone to check in with her a couple or more times a week like relatives in particular or a couple of good friends.

Previous to this time of being middle aged, she had been married twice and raised three children who were always very close with her. She survived her divorce quite well never submitting to emotional misery. She was always confident and secure within and even a little cocky about it.

Through those middle aged years, she met a nice man and became somewhat meaningfully involved without letting him know he was number one in her life. That bothered him because he thought he "was" number one after time had passed.

All seemed ordinary for awhile. Then Sharon decided she didn't want a commitment to one person because she could rely on her friends and relatives for security. She really wasn't so secure as to live without her people in her life.

Sharon broke it off with George saying she couldn't live with anyone. He treated her as well as anyone could or would, but she was determined to make it on her own having access to her very few friends and relatives fairly close at hand.

The years passed with her security on the teetering balance between her remaining relatives and being more alone than ever. Sharon and George communicated only as somewhat distant friends; nothing more.

Eventually, her remaining friends and relatives died or moved away and others just stopped communicating with her and she began falling victim to various annoying illnesses partly neurotic and partly organic because of her aging and abandonment. Further, she had to have help from doctors, emotional therapists and other medicare assistance.

Soon, she became immobile and into a wheelchair. She became progressively ill and reluctantly, but proudly, expressed her dismay of making impulsive errors in being so independent which were all due to her artificial security with family members. She was sinking into a doldrums of gloom and doom by herself and wished she had prepared herself differently. Her depression and illnesses progressed along with her set mannerisms. It was too late to change.

Sharon's case wasn't just the loss of her only real friend George who treated her and her family members dearly; she also, without much conscious awareness, suffered loss of her own ability to adapt and flex with what would eventually catch up with her; the misery of being alone, sick and close to helpless at the end of her life. One negative habit led to another.

Sharon was a case of not rising above her attitude that finally broke her down to a fateful and unrepenting victim of her own ignorance and doing.

We must be aware and preemptive when making serious mistakes in dealing with making more mistakes. It pays to be humble in making beneficial corrections in dealing with loss and corrections of those errors. Then we can handle loss better. Loss "does" happen in many different ways.

Rising above those errors in response to loss is best checked immediately after noticing the extremely emotional reactions so one can delete the adverse or undesirable programming and replace it with a satisfactory and more compatible program. Sure, it requires some dedicated effort. Anything worthwhile usually does. Even small dedications help to inspire more dedication and better life.

Rising above means conquering and that's just what it is; conquering the overbubbling or runaway emotions.

Knowing what can or what has become less or ineffectively controlled is a significant step in the preparation for controlling excessive emotional outbursts of which appear to hang on too long and annoy others at the same time.

Some people are aware of their emotional outbursts and want to subdue them and others refuse to listen or talk about them.

Those who are willing to look into those emotional reactions and talk about them have a fairly good chance to calm them down in the discussion and playacting scenes dealing with emotional strife and conflicting values etc. Group therapy, church groups, psychology classes and other methods mentioned in this book will contribute toward rising above the tendencies of overreacting to loss of any type.

If one is bent on living with the belief where expressive emotional flair to what appears a loss or even a disappointment cannot be regulated because it was inherited through family traits, may discover to be mistaken. Many family traits are simply a matter of one picking up the habits from another. Clinging to the cultured or genetic belief will "prevent" rising above the tendency to reduce the outbursts or uncontrolled mannerisms and feeling of grief or temperament. Those mannerisms are programmable neurotransmitting pathways of the brain receiving and placing suggestions into the subconscious mind. At that moment and in an ongoing time of programming, it forms the belief system, character and to some extent, personality that displays a representation of the individual's presentation of mind. Be careful of what is "fed" from the conscious part of the mind to the subconscious mind. When it goes in, it stays there and is mentally recorded for use in presenting oneself to the self "and" to others.

Want to be more accepted by others? Program better thoughts into your subconscious mind. That's the base of what you are in presenting yourself to others! Speaking to the self is subconscious programming and works wonders within.

The initial and strong contention of mind is akin to the argue oriented state of mind. Any very set state of mind emits a form of opinionated opposition called arguing and becomes resistant to change which in this case is whether or not to rise above the tendencies of overreacting during exposure to loss of any kind.

We are reaching a time in space on this earth when the people of the world are closing in on each other and are experiencing many disagreements that can trigger strife, clashing and hysteria. Not having our way through ego driven tendencies also becomes a form of loss. We need to control and contain our tendencies to "lose our cool" if we want peace, friends and continuously good relationships.

The best part of all this emotional containment is the characteristic of remaining calm which is a virtue of being compatible with any social situation and especially with the self.

Rising above grief and panic is available for everyone in, of course, variable degrees of desire, perception and value. We will go whichever way we lead ourselves.

Whichever way we lead ourselves deserves more "thought" than just doing it. We are daily, monthly and yearly programmed to be the way we are. That's important for us to consciously maintain awareness of (not forget). If we loose consciousness of that point, we will continue with our present program whether it serves us or not. Changing our programming for improved emotional stability requires realistically analyzing our present state of thinking, believing and whether "they" are serving us well or not. Then if they aren't, we must devise a new program, as mentioned, into our brain and let it become an integral part of our psychological makeup by constantly reviewing it vocally day by day. It's like they always say, "Use it or lose it." Programming the young adapts quicker and lasts longer without as much emphasis on the discipline of practice. Getting older requires more time practicing the art of reprogramming. This all adds to rising above adverse reaction to loss. One must allot time for this valuable development.

All life long is a constant series of pleasures, challenges, rewards and unfortunately, problems, set backs and demotions galore. Taking, receiving or how about becoming a victim of unfavorable breaks or circumstances which seemed like a form of losing at the time can be classified as losses very easily if allowed.

If we believe we are subjected to the concept of losing or becoming a victim of having something or someone taken away or "lost" by the wayside in the shuffle of everyday life, we can then become the unfortunate recipient of cultural logic and suggestion. That is what was relayed to us by parents, teachers, philosophers, employers, religions and a host of other preacher type insinuators of which can be traditionally understood as negative propelled emotion.

We can further support that tradition of feeling terrible in response or we can choose to eliminate it from our belief system and rise above its old time magnetism of which humans are attempting in so many manners while not even realizing its influence.

No one has to suffer traditionally inflicted remorse or other emotional pain from culturally derived logic; that is, how we have been taught to respond. When and if it happens, take hold, be aware of it cutting in to the calm status quo. Remember these guidelines and practice them. The pain will be much less, maybe even less than that.

One last reminder in this chapter, rising above adverse reactions of what we think and believe of as loss requires developing a belief where the "feelings" of loss are "only" emotional reactions and not really attached with or to anything bad or so terrible like it "seems" at the time.

Chapter 9

Loss can trigger innovation for creative progress and goals

$\mathcal{W}$hen losing something or someone seems so much a part of us, it's like they will never be replaced or happen again and is almost unbearable. It sometimes seems as though life has slowed to a worthless and nonprogressive existence. Of course the opposite can occur too as wanting to compensate for the loss by inquiring even more into what seemed to be lost. That's a healthy state of mind. So, whether it's an exciting gain of some kind or a striking realization of losing something or someone, life "does" continue to be either "down in the dumps," as they say, or a rebound that snaps one back into the usual or even better order of the day.

Jon's immediate family was the only solid home base he ever had for feeling secure and stable. His kids left home in their teens and shortly his wife chose to have her own life and departed. Jon didn't have friends he could depend on and was pretty much alone beside his work.

Jon became involuntarily despondent and led himself in directions that might make him feel better. It didn't work. His remaining friends couldn't helpfully face him for any period of time in his depressed state of emotional insufficiency. He couldn't eat or sleep and began to deteriorate at a still young middle age.

Jon began to play tennis. That didn't help. He went to organized singles parties. That didn't get it. He even tried a little drinking, smoking and dope. That made it worse. After those unrewarding experiences and along with never having any meaningful or authoritative guidance, he decided to do something for someone else other than his own sad self. He did some volunteer work for a church that participated in social improvement programs. He became interested in various social/therapy groups and without anyone telling him, discovered there was much more to life than the psychological restrictions and confinement of domesticated family life of which was about all he knew. He flung himself into the study of interpersonal and business relationships and how to achieve compatibility with one another. He became an emotional therapist since he personally and educationally experienced so much emotional misery in his own life. That allowed him to understand how other people might feel and was an example of creative opportunity when loss presents it.

Jon apparently had to "hit the bottom," so to speak and almost desperately "reached out" for some form of guidance to acquire a self-sufficient strength to survive, be accepted and maybe even be admired as a result of those progressive accomplishments. Now he is a business consultant on subjects pertaining to the progress of self-improvement.

Many people have to pass through wasted years of misery after loss or repeated losses making their personal situations of loss even worse through being too set in their ways and not adhering to suggestions of improvement and change. Experiences of misery "do" add toward the value of understanding how "others" feel in the same predicament if one will choose to view it in that manner.

One might go so far as to say there are some "candidates" who will adopt and adhere to change and improvements in their emotional stability of mind. Furthermore, they may be willing to spread similar possibilities to others who may be setting up resistance against adaptation to changing their stance on loss or defensive mannerisms.

Step lightly, though, in helping others in a nonprofessional manner. There are times when those who are rock hard set in their ways can be resentful, incoherent, defensive and as much as psychotic in response to what may be good intentions to help them. They may interpret help as dangerous or mischievous. Help works much better when they indicate they need it or, better still, ask for it. Setting a good example "is" help to some degree. Remember, in a safe environment, the practicing teacher usually learns more than the student.

Everyone has, at least, an opportunity to experience a more comfortable and contented state of mind thereby acquiring physical improvements as well. They both work together and one can enhance the other, generally speaking.

Once again, as an added benefit for those who may be inspired or even for those who may not be so inspired, as we age (and that can mean any numbers), one of "the" most important assurances we can appreciate is to possess a resolved and contented peace and comfort of mind. An emotionally impulsive and resistantly or hysterically triggered reaction to anything or anybody considered as a loss or "a hit to the ego" may be interpreted as an attack or rebellion within the self. That's grounds for emotional upheaval and psychological imbalance which is not particularly a healthy state of existance for maintaining a progressively rewarding life into the future. If that possibility can be realistically viewed and accepted by the accused, the emotional course of defensive and extreme reaction to the perception of loss will be more favorably ready for change. It may be important enough in the aspect of surviving by virtue of one's personal attitude.

Much can be said for the value of learning how to adopt and adapt to a reliable philosophy and system of rational behavior with already present guidelines. Adding to that, one can benefit from actually experiencing and hanging on to the misery of grief from loss and creatively pass it on to others who are reaching out in their awkward or objective ways. Rewards of sincerely sharing experiences, acquired knowledge and solutions on reducing or overcoming these defensive and extreme loss reactions are endless. The knowledge acquired from it all is priceless and available. The time and effort put forth in searching to develop these strengths will reward those who are perseverantly interested and willing to pursue them.

Gathering reason, desire and momentum for setting goals in triggering this innovation of helping others to manage loss better will be a valuable asset in the progress of the self to do the same. Like they say, what moves around comes around.

Whenever one experiences a very sudden loss, that can allow new emotional strength for one who has had many losses of significant magnitude which can also result in a growing depression. Which way it develops depends on the nature of its programming and the length of time it becomes vested. Some people become very set in those habitual mannerisms and others have had training and/or exposure to changing and adapting for improving their lifestyle and mental health. It's a matter of how a person either ignores the tendencies in remaining the same or will initiate changes for improvement. Goals and choosing are available and there is plenty of it.

Don't ever let it be said or thought loss of any kind is final where life will never be the same again as far as feeling good or even great after the estranged incident occurred. Life may be different, but originally, those situations attracted what became a loss. They did it before. They can do it again as long as one doesn't crawl into a hole, so to speak, of unexposure thinking that's the way to recover from the loss. Face it head on with new innovation and goals and new strength will accompany those efforts.

Being innovative more than ever gets relief, among other methods, from the blues, pains and fatigue of emotional loss symptoms. It works like anything else works when its faced head on and realistically.

Once again, there are plenty of choices, goals and alternatives for relief from loss agony. Continue to notice them in these texts. Don't let the loss blues eat you up! If you do, there won't be much left for living an enjoyable life into the future.

Chapter 10

Loss as increments of development

*F*urther understanding of loss to resolve it is coupled with not only the forward or backward perception of change and progress, which some may refer to as positive or negative, but with the actual manner of approach concerning the direction toward achieving that knowledge.

Understanding the reaction to loss becomes availably easy at the time of the loss when one's emotions take over and speak loudly that somebody or something isn't there anymore as, "I've been robbed" or "What will I do now?" Those questions can instinctively tell a person what the most important response is at the time of the noticed loss.

However and unfortunately, the untrained mind is so hectically emotional at that time, it cannot clearly see the opportunity of understanding how to overcome the grief.

What is a little more difficult to immediately grasp onto, if at all, is how to understand how to go about understanding what may appear as "unreal" to accept, perceive and rationally deal with. That happens, many times, because others do the same thing especially at a death scene. That inability to understand how to understand is also experienced with the loss of material things or a job etc. where empathy, sympathy, pity and other feelings of being sorry are displayed to the victim of loss which can be even more confusing and disillusioning. Usually, that victim of loss can only handle one sorryful response. Getting too much sympathy etc. "can" be received as forcing one to feel better. That doesn't work too well.

Understanding how to understand is accomplished in increments over a period of time. Progress of all people and other living species unfolds with some adapting quickly, some normally and others requiring more time to sort out their reasoning for understanding. Sure, it's like any other subject to be learned, absorbed and maintained; only more from the emotionally viewed approach.

Understanding how to understand the self's emotional reactions is a "development" of gathered ideas, ideals, principles, feelings, objectives and other factors adding to what the noticed "and" unnoticed character is of that self. Those factors must be studied and extrapolated for broadening the scope in this area of loss grief. It "is" well worth the effort.

The discipline of patience during the initial reaction needs to be high on the list of priorities necessary for "developing" and understanding how to understand and is done in increments of time, not immediately. Strength of emotional stability doesn't happen that quick. Patience is needed.

Everything we learn about our environment and living beings inhabiting it adds toward understanding a great deal of it and interrelating with it. That's one form of developing with it all. That development includes notches of exposure to as much as possible, blending with or against it and/or taking chances and risks or not. Regardless of whether it is all about being for or contrary in the development, development is still an incremental growth as a plus, minus, positive or negative no matter which direction may be the stronger tendency or choice.

Another aspect of development with anything is how we continuously choose to identify and adapt our inner selves when interrelating with others or things.

The conscious combination of incrementally developing with internal awareness experiences and external awareness experiences will help allow one to further understand why and how one "is" understanding in the present and whether one wants to or even "can" make changes in the development of understanding. Several judgmental perceptions of good, bad, right or wrong add toward the individualistic rationale of understanding the how, what and why of understanding.

The essence of understanding any incremental progress in the development of that understanding is the key to a wider perspective of total understanding for the sheer benefit of internal acceptance, increased self-esteem and more rewarding social adaptation etc. for gaining control over loss vulnerability. Another way to describe it is as follows:

Focusing on the more perspective view of understanding is the ongoing objective for what needs to be understood, but the bigger picture is only a sum total of all the little things gathered, perceived and developed. So, developing "for" expanding the perspective is better handled beforehand with gathered incremental (several) progress. Doing it all at once may be detrimental to the cause.

While all this progress of handling loss better continues, practice taking loss as though it is a grain of salt. That will be easier to begin with. It's all about being cool, calm and collected.

Sure, we all want things to happen right now and tend to lose interest or get sidetracked by what may seem more important for latching onto. Actually, what could be more important than developing and preserving a more comfortable state of thinking and feeling? That's something to put on the front burner, if you will, for our future of "being" cool, calm, collected and strong in every encounter of life.

Everything we do in this life unfolds as some kind of development. A business, a marriage, building a house, having an education, you name it. When a woman gets pregnant, that has to be the most natural development of them all and requires no skill at all. Imagine the state of mind a woman would exist in if she thought it would be too much to handle or if she had to remember all the details of maternity or if she had to practice having a baby; all before she allowed the fertility process to occur?

Some of the most meaningful, heart touching and yes, emotionally taxing experiences one can have only require the knowledge of being patient, calm and crossing each bridge of time in their natural order; definitely not attempting to "make" or "force" a weary and uncomfortable feeling change its natural course. Some of those feelings of losing someone or something are simply increments of development in forming a preparation for more natural life of maybe more of a similar nature. It all adds to part of life; nothing really any more than that. Be patient with increments of loss agony.

Also, where one is resistant to natural instinct, it may be helpful to realize there is a choice in developing the necessary increments of knowledge that reduces anxiety supporting instability.

Chapter 11

Can a loss really become a gain?

$\mathcal{O}$ne who has just suffered a loss may consider this title a little misleading as a big farce or fantasy where a loss can be a gain. Let's see if it's true, false or whatever else; things not always being as they seem.

Bertram went sky diving one day. Prior to the dive, he planned on landing on a hill and brush area. The day of his jump, the pilot of the plane climbed high in his coordinated route and had calculated the direction of the wind for ejecting out. Momentarily, they couldn't see the landing spot. Bertram jumped with all the precautionary moves and away he went enjoying his trip in the air. He descended through the planned route and noticed a brushfire exactly where he was to land, so to avoid possible burning upon landing, he released his parachute and pulled it into a guiding position away from the landing spot. Using his parachute as a sail, he sped up his descending move. It did turn his direction just enough to avoid the fire, but alas, this control of the parachute meant he was descending at a much faster rate of speed and would hit the ground at a neck breaking speed. Fortunately, with his pulling and pushing and a lucky wind, he was able to jockey his panic made craft over into a small lake. He doubled up in a tight fetus like position and with a mighty punch into the water, he sank deeply in without hitting the bottom. He arose somewhat stunned, but conscious and survived the ordeal.

Bertram was energy drained, relieved and really quite proud of his very possible loss that turned into an amazing gain with his close objective, his dignity and possibly his sustained life.

A little luck and a little skill was certainly helpful along with his lust and drive to make it work. Making anything work as well as possible is, many times, better than only hoping it will work as planned. His primary objective was to survive.

Maybe other situations dealing with emotional grief will be less hazardous and easier to attain as a gain resulting from a possible loss where objective and calm approach is exercised. Other situations of possible loss can be avoided with a little or more training in emotional control utilized as preventive measures. They can save us from many embarrassing disappointments.

Ricardo was the studio's worst student dancer. At the time, all he wanted to do was become an outstanding dancer and to be accepted as someone with a title and good reputation with his skills. He stumbled and fumbled in his dance instructions to the point of frustration, embarrassment and eventually walking out the door. When his ego came back into balance, he gathered a stronger desire to be a subject of his dance fantasy. He still appeared as a loser in dancing and because of his knowing it attended dances galore just to watch. While he watched with his mind's eye, he mentally soaked up as many dance moves as he could. He took it all home and secretly pretended he had a dance partner where he practiced as much as he could remember and then some. He was profoundly determined to learn, practice and prove how good he could be with fancy dancing.

Ricardo returned to the studio and after his class lesson practiced what he learned with one of the other students. Along with what he remembered watching at the dances and practicing at home, it gave him the needed confidence necessary to offset his feelings of dance inadequacy.

Before long, he acquired a steady dance partner and studied dance with her while sharing what he had learned. Over the months "and" years, they both excelled in dancing and became competition dancers who were quite well known in their circles.

What Ricardo originally "thought" was a losing game turned into a successful gain through desire, awareness, confrontation and determination along with the magnetisms of his newly and optimistically driven skills and willingness to learn. This is an example of how the seemingly down and out can turn into the up and in; even with odds of which didn't seem favorable at the time.

One last example of what could almost be referred to as a metamorphic transformation of loss into a gain where Angie had a subjected nature to be ill (losing health) and turned it into a very successful gain of robust health as follows:

Angie was little and underweight as a child. She was vulnerable to several childhood illnesses. Her immune system was under par. This happened "before" the advent of aids, so there was no connection. It continued throughout her younger life and the future of her health didn't look too bright.

Even though she ate fairly normal, she was weak like a third bird in a nest. She loved to be active in sports and other physical activity, but her stamina was low and could only excel for awhile. She became tired easily.

Angie lived with her eccentric grandmother who was more concerned about her own self than Angie. Angie had to handle her own problems herself like so many others have had to do including your author who had very similar experiences as noted in the listed publication of "Staying Alive On Planet Earth #1." As Angie grew a little older, she discovered her problems must have been do to the food and liquid she consumed among other toxic exposures that was making her ill, so she rearranged a strict diet along with certain environmental restrictions and improved hygienic habits and began using vitamin supplements as she learned more about them.

When Angie escaped the domination of her grandmother and accepted more responsibility for herself, she had medical and wholistic examinations taken including allergy tests. She discovered she was a victim of several food allergies, their combinations and the consumption of uncontrolled acidic food.

Angie became even more strict with her health habits which improved steadily as time passed, but there was still no weight gained until one doctor discovered she had lived with an underlying condition of depression possibly for years. She began a treatment of a calming formula. It reduced anxiety thereby calmed her system down and allowed a better appetite for gaining a reasonable amount of weight to her frail body of which she was continuously able to control by regulating the amount of her formula.

Angie may have withered away over time had it not been for her relentless efforts to make changes in so many ways so she could be proud of herself and her gains. She became a good example for others to follow. She did it "her" way with calm, logical methods of trial and error. More currently than in the past, there is more of this type of accessible information that saves time in stumbling through mistakes of trial and error.

These examples are expressed to say losses have always had their opportunities to become gains of some nature. Whenever there is a war, for instance, it's amazing how people rebuild their societies back up even bigger and better than before. Usually, when we lose someone, we gain someone else or even many more especially when we nourish that possibility and choose to believe it. Belief is not only powerful, but a very good friend and asset to rely on "when" nourishing it. Losing something or an ability can also be supplemented with alternatives as long as we have even a spark of desire. One spark can grow into lighting up a display or even a chain reaction of new light and insight for expounding on it.

We can gain from "any" loss as long as we are alive. Loss can be perceived as a mere lesson on how to deal with other unforeseen circumstances. That's a gain. Besides, getting a little emotionally tougher won't hurt a thing. It builds confidence for further living purposes. More confidence and emotional strength is what follows. That statement isn't just a cheap opinion. It's the experience your author has encountered through practicing the enclosed methods and acquired beliefs of offsetting loss grief. It get's constantly better with the many times mentioned effort and patience.

Yes, a loss can be something that hasn't gained any momentum yet and may be considered a loss even with all its attempts. Loss isn't always after the fact of its existence. Sometimes people feel like they aren't getting anywhere no matter what they do. That could be referred to as constant preloss. What can they do about it?

First, they have to get off the stick of being stuck in bad habits by creating a diversion of some kind that makes them look into a mirror of themselves to realize the seriousness where change is needed. A diversion from the routine can be to join a therapy group through or at a church, a city or community health center or at various business and more privately advertised emotional therapy groups. Any groups where people gather to share meaningful feedback to one another for helping to realize possible improvements are a plus. One can express feelings of instability and weaknesses in a safe environment and ask questions etc. There are all types of people at these groups to stimulate the consciousness for change. Then devise a plan and goals for gaining emotional control similar to what is being studied here. These groups are inexpensive and may be enough for one's cause as compared to more educated and polished professionals. Take your pick.

Chapter 12

Loss in perspective

$\mathcal{O}$ne could say, "A loss is just a loss. What's the big deal?" As we can see now, one loss "can" lead the mind and following body to other and more losses if we refuse to be creative in reaction to some of them. For instance, we hear and see so much in the news of people simply disagreeing which leads to yelling, fighting and consequently killing someone when there could have been an ego restraining action that prevented the worst scenario action.

The guys in a local bar were drinking beer, laughing and joking like a typical group exercising their vocal expressions. One of them (Hal) became defensively upset because one of his rivals was using humor to precariously aggravate and discredit him, he "thought." He couldn't resist the temptation to fight, but the other guy was bigger and stronger and Hal wasn't physically equipped to compete with him.

Someone else may have just dismissed that aggravation without a severe ego reaction, laughed it off and let it go as group fun, but not Hal. He wasn't accustomed to being discredited and with the combination of being somewhat inebriated and angry, he dismissed himself, went out and prepared a Molotov cocktail (small fire bomb), returned to the bar and while "flipping his lid," threw it into the crowd where his rival was sitting. It was a disastrous scene and he was imprisoned for a very long time.

When Hal's defense mechanisms and anger emanated, even though it was influenced and possibly triggered by alcohol and the other guy, it wasn't anyone elses decision to proceed with his belligerent attack. It was only "his."

If Hal had "any" preconceived ideas of what he may have lost in that episode, there is a better chance than not he could have psychologically prepared his defensive nature where it could have offset his tendency to lose his cool. An example of that statement: One might say, "I had a taste of what it was like being in jail overnight, so I will never do anything that may put me there again." That loss of freedom was an opportunity which justified reason to use preventive methods for staying out of jail and other trouble too in relationship with being so confined. Previous insight pays.

Tendencies for humans are to become educated for surviving with the value and adaptation to having money, another person or more, a job, a home, a car, food, water, conventional knowledge and various safety factors etc. What they miss, many times, is the necessity of purposely preparing themselves for unaware surprises and certain adverse circumstances lurking. Auto accidents are typical. Who thinks ahead of the possibility they may be involved in an auto accident when driving to work? That's only for "other" people one may think. Actually "being" in an accident can be almost incomprehensible. So what happens? They don't strategically, characteristically or emotionally prepare themselves for such an event and when it "does" happen, it becomes an almost demoralizing experience depending, of course, on the degree of destruction and it's intensity. Remaining "aware" of possible losses is preventive practice.

Schools and fire departments etc. manage to be quite objective, rational, calm and collected in emergency situations because of their preparing for it. The common layman "could" adopt a mentality capable of preventing irrational decisions, panic situations and poor judgment at the moment among many other preventable mistakes. Furthermore, most of those or other adverse situations could be avoided by, as mentioned, "opening up" emotionally and verbally to those who have common interests in groups of communicative therapy for the purpose of exchanging views which leads to making changes in perception, perspective and attitudes concerning rigid, one way thinking, concepts of programming and top priority of reprogramming the mind which subsequently forms a renewed character on one's choices. Then, life becomes more rationally and emotionally manageable while easier to endure along with the new and enhanced social and romantic attributes, whatever they may be.

Anyone who unreservedly expresses critical and emotional feelings concerning loss is usually contrary minded at that time even in that person's social circle and usually lives with self-centered views. Those rigid views don't include a respect of opinions, thoughts, ideas and viewpoints of others. The results unfold with incompatible reactions, nonacceptance, misunderstanding (sometimes irreversible), personality clashing plus undesirable demands and expectations of others.

Viewing everybody and everything in our world now as incommunicably far away is a deceiving and detrimental distraction. Everything and everybody "are" drawing closer together with the population expansion. We will inevitably fight each other or join in mutual recognition where we must exchange with one another. The latter "can" happen just as well as the former. Presently, there are signs of both potentials.

Squabbling and fighting results from imperialistic or higher than thou attitudes or defensive and retributive beliefs and aggression. We can control both now more than ever because of our intellectually acquired patience, perception and preventive methods which are available for utilizing.

Our extended knowledge to be compatible with one another through the medium of exchanging material goods, services, love and sharing ideas etc. with each other as compared to taking them away from each other by force is favorable by most people of the world. They are just not practicing enough of it. Let us all do it and set better examples to follow.

Only cartels, monopolistic regimes and other indoctrinational conglomerates get involved in the highly competitive "dog eat dog" directors of push, shove, connive and care less about anyone else's losses. That appears to be and has been the reality of humanity for as long as we have known in the past.

The majority of the world's people are what makes them tick. Everything starts and ends with "their" attitudes toward one another. Individuals will always be the one's who will inevitably make the philosophies of change through insight, choice, common rallies, pain and greed. Most of these people live their lives through representative power of conglomerates and want peace, but are not willing to study personality and character differentiation. They just want things their own individualistic way. No wonder there are world wide conflicts. Everyone cannot have their own way all the time, except within their own selves.

Your author prefers to believe when "individuals," more than conglomerates, become more aware of which route social compatibility "can" lead, they will work more extensively on their individual selves along with others in "supporting" the causes of being good examples of emotional and rational stability in an exchanging manner instead of "This is the way it is; take it or leave it" attitude. Then our perception and reaction to this thing we call loss will become less emphatic, less devastating and less of a burden emotionally and all around. The artificial and euphoric view of conquering and dominating won't be exercised and will become outdated.

Everything in this pro or con euphoria hinges on the choice, effort and willingness of the individual, not primarily the city, state, national government or private enterprise. We've always known the vote of the people is powerful. The power of the individual to develop respect and caring for others as well as the self will spread as examples to others and will inevitably become powerfully influential to world leaders. Loss will then become less and easier to endure.

Sure, it may sound like pure fantasy to some and possible, but not likely to others. The skeptics and pessimists are always around. We need their input too for balance purposes. They may not "be" as skeptical and pessimistic as we preconceivably judge them. They have their story too.

However, even if the whole world doesn't adopt this optimistic view and work toward it, whoever does adopt these ways of self-improvement will certainly and largely benefit from them in ways of self-acceptance, self-esteem, being a good example and a host of other social, healthful, emotional and extra acceptional manners. They all add to emotional stability.

The more we delve into legitimate self-improvement, the more we improve our relationships with everyone and all situations. Sincerity and flexibility with the self, others and a cause will almost always prevail for being more stable.

Comparing the successes and failures, which may be considered gains and losses to some degree of the past, we are understanding the larger majority of successes weren't so much a matter of luck as much as they were a matter of being prepared. Sometimes we spend a lot of time goofing off, shirking responsibility and procrastinating. We might just as well invest some of that time in preparing against not so desirable "effects" of failure or loss. We are also learning failure and loss sprints alongside success and gain. That is real. One teaches the other and they are both available just like love and hate are so closely related. Yes, they both cause tears.

The odds favor success and gain where learned skill, noncontradiction, diligence and sincerity are exercised. The failure/loss syndrome is simply an instinctually and socially programmed emotional reaction from traditional and existing influence and not much of anything else.

Loss is conventionally believed as not owning it anymore, but the concept is rather erroneous because we cannot take anything or anybody with us when we die; therefore things and people are only utilized, not really owned. Ownership can be conceived as forever. Nothing is forever and proof of that is in the universe. Nothing, in the long run, is continuous.

Everything rotates and changes through the space of time. Once again, why would we be any different in possessing or "keeping."

We need to perceptively and perspectively collect our values of living, relating and reacting to whatever experiences we encounter whether they are planned, circumstantial or an unexpected surprise that pops into our laps so we can much easier manage these reactions and reactions to reactions.

Final analysis reveals, at least in this book, the sorrowful feelings experienced with the loss of anything or anybody is indeed a perfectly normal phenomenon. Separating the reactionary feeling of the loss (the emotional weakening) from the actual thing or living being (what is gone) has a tendency to lighten the heavy feeling of anxiety and grieving. Many times, separating the loss of an actual job of employment, for instance, from the devastating feelings following the job termination can relieve overburdening anxiety that can cause further emotional reactions by just letting it be how it is. Fretting only makes it worse.

One can offset the annoying feelings of loss by some or more preparing anytime; especially when loss hasn't happened yet. Both gain and loss will be around as long as we are alive. When we die, it will vanish too. The individual can whip the unpleasantly overbearing feelings of loss and reap in the advantages incurred with them before the adverse feelings of loss whips the individual. Determination gets it. Get up and go!

Remember, once again in a little different manner, when the loss happens, it becomes nonexistant. It is over and done. The loss cannot return. Technically, the loss per se, cannot "do" anything to the person unless it's an encounter of physical damage. It is only the recipient of the loss or better stated, the one who has chosen to be the recipient of the loss who affects or even injures that individual's feelings, nothing or anyone else.

The individual's mind is that which control's the individual's feelings, not the loss itself.

Depart from being self-victimized and feel better for moving into new or other territory—unless the "loss" isn't or wasn't really perceived as a loss at all and only looked at as something of which has "changed." Change has been around a long time.

The most important aspect and requirement for controlling emotional reactions to "anything" is to exercise patience even if it means utilizing strict discipline in managing that patience. Calm "will" unfold with patience supported by at least "some" discipline. Anger at loss is only psychobiologic energy burning as it is a detriment in maintaining good health and longevity. Long live the king of being calm.

The loss psychologically incurred by an individual is only emotionally justified as a loss to be proven as such by self-inflicted pain. It isn't really necessary to suffer loss so much if at all.

There is no conceptual or intrinsic value to the meaning of loss. It has been traditionally accepted in a take away aspect and has resulted in an unhappy feeling or incomplete fulfillment. Do we want or expect that to dominate us?

However, one must not generalize as loss being permanent. It is only a state of existence for a period of time and can be better accepted as such than a devastating permanency of which one may derail one's lust for life. After all, that lust is what we are here for with all the trimmings wherever possible. Once again, don't let the magnetism of loss drain you down.

The balance of this book has been designed mainly for raising the consciousness/awareness of individuals who desire a more meaningful and efficient state of emotional stability of which one can depend on for feeling better concerning adapting with the everyday and future experiences of life where keeping a "cool" head is so necessary in flowing compatibly with all that is plentifully offered in this life.

One thing "does" usually lead to another as a reminder for choosing the route to go. The good things in life are immensely available. Why not put out some effort and "allow" us all to come together with calm and patience as a way of life while loss emotions become more compatibly endured? Loss is only a change. Don't be "bummed out" by changes. That's only a part of life.

Your author, Lloyd E. McIlveen unveils a chronological list of many and various book subjects presenting controversial, educational, uplifting, futuristic, self-helping, philosophical, psychological, entertaining and other stimulating concepts of which are and will be displayed with brief descriptions of each book as follows:

1. "Evaluating Outdated Beliefs" This is a report, viewed through the perception of your author of the evolutionary process and changes occurring in belief; especially in the area of religion and spirituality. This was designed for the benefit of broadening individual perception, perspective and viewing "another" plane of belief while revealing fallacies in theological indoctrination. This is an improved revision of the book's origin.

2. "Staying Alive On Planet Earth I" This is a psychology of health required to stabilize and maintain better health for the benefit of

living a much longer life. Source: A lifetime of study, problems, recoveries and many successes more in natural methods.

3. "Understanding Loss To Relieve The Anguish" Loss of anything involves many distractions and disrupting emotional disarray. Gaining greater understanding of these emotions offsets the misery of them and enhances optimism of confidence and support for emotional weakness before, at and during the time of loss.

4. "Understanding Preventing And Eliminating Cancer" presents new views on the wonders of natural methods for practical use.

5. "Paradox Of Progress Unfolding I" This is a tale told by a man "many" centuries into the future about an exciting, overwhelming and terrifying occurrence on planet Earth as a result of their wondrous progress around the time of 2300 A.D. Hang onto your seats! #2 is a second issue later on the list.

6. "Offsetting Climate Change And Nuclear Waste Contamination" This view of the two exposes the hazards, inevitabilities and possible solutions needed now for preventing a "too late" disaster that will affect all living beings too soon.

7. "What God Is And Is Not" This is a study of spiritual possibilities designed, not particularly to remold conventional mannerisms of belief, but to open and expand perception in the most controversial subject of mankind; the subject of God and whether mankind will or won't expand that consciousness along with all progress and growth on Earth and in the universe.

8. "Kids Of The Crick" This is a story of four old fashioned country kids setting out on a weekend adventure in their countryside of tall grass, mountains, rivers, animals, caves and strange living beings. Sometimes, they aren't sure whether it's all real or not.

9. "Paradox Of Destiny Explained" eliminates the mysteries, facades, fantasies and deceptions of how, where, way and when we do what we do and opens new possibilities for expanding our beliefs and consciousness pertaining to this study of available options that may influence insight for growth, change or even justify present mannerisms of what may control the individual, planet Earth or the whole universe and is not zealous, fanatic or bigoted; only assertively revealing.

10. "Paradox Of Progress Unfolding 2" This book is a continued fiction story and can be considered exemplary of "major" human changes that alienated millions of people to another planet in the future. They are led by the elements of unexpected surprises of which is par for the course with gutsy space pioneers. The first "Paradox Of Progress Unfolding I" must be read first to understand and appreciate the disproportional attitudes

and positions of people on a threshold of major change and disasters upon them. This is not only a tale of travel, trials and tribulations, it is philosophically stimulating and adds toward future insightful expansion of the human species.

11. "Staying Alive On Planet Earth 2" This is all extended version of the original psychology of health for living a longer life. More knowledge allows more life.

12. "Preventing The Doom Of Mankind" This is a stimulating, vitalizing and somewhat shocking description of how mankind is "truly" faced with extinction in the "near" future due to their own faults of progress. It's very educational and needed now to help offset that inevitability where the odds dictate we will all perish if we don't adhere to this offsetting of which "is" possible to achieve.

13. "Spiritual Transformation Of The Fourth Millennium" Old-time conventional religion

is fading. New-time spirituality is on the rise. Objective realism is the prime issue here for future inclined thinking and believing.

14. "Understanding The Science Of Creative Mind" This is a study for discovering, developing and practicing a psychological powerhouse within for conquering the unconquerable, achieving the impossible or doing things no one has done all depending on, of course, the makeup and determination of the individual. This study brings out a greater potential of the individual's abilities when taken seriously. This was compiled from a lifetime of study and experience from your author.

15. "Living to 150" is a guidance program for intentions of anyone desiring a longer than longer life which is insightfully and innovatively educational for that purpose.

16. "The Act Of Getting One's Act Together" If anyone, business or nation wants to develop their stance, priorities and position in life, this

is a chance for them to get their act together more than ever.

17. "Making Changes From This Point Forward" The design of this book is for the purpose of preventing repeated mistakes of unforeseen surprises due to what we weren't or aren't aware of that did, can or will happen again. It's all about gaining or rearranging change consciousness in this area.

18. "Relationships For All" This is a carefully arranged view of how relationships can function much better when initiated or guided by the experiences of many experts and your author who have had failures and successes in their very human encounters. The experiences of more relationships result in wiser judgments and approaches to others.

19. "The We Between Us" helps us in discovering who is good for us and who is not. First it is a study in the book. Then

it is a study with people of what exists in two party's minds (individuals business or nations) when first confronted. A real time saver in evaluating possible compatibility or not between the two for anyone. It works.

20. "Passion Of Dance" This is a narrative on progress, value and guidance for the dance inclined. It's informative and inspiring with its history and recent magnetism.

21. "Open That Door" to love. This book is comprehensively all about love. It's not a storybook. It clears up the differences of love that causes misunderstanding, suspicion and deception.

22. "Get The Spirit" This book describes controversial and somewhat intertwined conventional views of spirit, spirits and spirituality. This book untangles the "usual" views and presents a more perspective manner of living with these concepts of mind.

23. "Stories Of What They Couldn't Or Wouldn't Tell" Ages are from babies to 100 years; twenty four of them.

24. "Improving On Love And Relationships" This one is two books in one. Part one "Open That Door" is a psychology of love that enhances perspective to understand and adapt to a very popular, but deceiving, repressed and ignored emotion; love. Part two covers "Relationships For All" which elaborates on origination, different types, significance, deceptions, desires, experiences, communication, possibilities, future and guidance of relationships. It's comprehensive and also derived from a lifetime of relationship experiences and serious study.

INDEX